BLOODY History of America

AMERICA'S BLOODY HISTORY FROM VIETNAM TO THE WAR ON TERROR

BLOODY History of America

AMERICA'S BLOODY HISTORY FROM VIETNAM TO THE WAR ON TERROR

KIERON CONNOLLY

Enslow Publishing
101 W. 23rd Street
Suite 240
New York, NY 10011
USA

enslow.com

This edition published in 2018 by:

Enslow Publishing, LLC
101 W. 23rd Street, Suite 240
New York, NY 10011

Cataloging-in-Publication Data
Names: Connolly, Kieron.
Title: America's bloody history from Vietnam to the war on terror / Kieron Connolly.
Description: New York : Enslow Publishing, 2018. | Series: Bloody history of America | Includes bibliographical references and index.
Identifiers: ISBN 9780766091801 (library bound) | ISBN 9780766095564 (pbk.)
Subjects: LCSH: Vietnam War, 1961-1975—Juvenile literature.| War on Terrorism, 2001-2009—Juvenile literature. | United States—History—1945-—Juvenile literature.
Classification: E741 .C5749 2018 | DDC 973.92—dc23

Printed in China

To Our Readers: We have done our best to make sure all websites in this book were active and appropriate when we went to press. However, the author and the publisher have no control over and assume no liability for the material available on those websites or on any websites they may link to. Any comments or suggestions can be sent by email to customerservice@enslow.com.

Photo Credits: Cover (left), pp. 3 (left), 6 Bettmann/Getty Images; cover (right), p. 3 (right) Getmilitaryphotos/Shutterstock.com; Alamy: 24 (World History Archive), 76 (David Grossman); Alamy/Everett Collection: 29, 41; Cody Images: 14, 15, 25; Dreamstime: 57 (Jgorzynik), 75 (Joshua Haviv); Getty Images: 11 (Hulton), 12 (Keystone-France), 26 (Hulton), 32 (Bill Owers/20th Century Fox), 33 (Henry Groskinsky/Life), 38 (Hulton), 42 (Horacio Villalobos), 44 (Hulton), 45 (Gjon Mili/Life), 49 (Frank Johnston/The Washington Post), 52 (Mike Evers/AFP) 59 (Peter Turnley), 60 (Ted Soqui), 62 (Sygma/Elizabeth Baranyai), 63 (Gregory Smith), 65 (Stephen J. Boitano), 69 (Spencer Platt), 72 (Tom Pennington), 74 (New York Daily News Archive), 78 (Jim Watson); Getty Images/Archive Photos: 10; Getty Images/Bettmann: 31, 36, 37, 39, 46; Library of Congress: 17; NASA: 51; U.S. Department of Defense: 18, 21, 66; White House: 71 (Peter Souza).

CONTENTS

American soldiers were deployed to Southeast Asia in the mid-twentieth century during the Vietnam War. Advances in technology and chemical warfare coupled with more conventional tactics created distinct horrors for all those near the conflict, both soldiers and civilians alike.

INTRODUCTION

IN MORE RECENT CHAPTERS OF AMERICAN HISTORY, MANY OF THE ISSUES THE US has faced have been similar to ones seen before, though they have evolved with advances in technology, domestic society, and foreign policy, too.

In the 1960s, America became embroiled in an increasingly unpopular war fighting communism in Vietnam. Massive protests took place at home, uniting people of different backgrounds in antiwar sentiment and occasionally turning deadly. During this period, violence also entered America by way of political assassinations, and a shaken US government navigated many troubling circumstances in the aftermath. Corruption in the Nixon administration resulted in the first resignation of a US president and became a touchstone for the American political climate even today.

In the decades that followed, a sense of a fractured society fostered complex cases, like the rise of cult leaders Charles Manson and David Koresh, complicating criminal justice in unprecedented ways. Gun violence spread across the country and still occurs in the US on a daily basis, manifesting in the forms of police shootings and, less commonly, mass attacks carried out by different kinds of terrorists. The concept of terrorism became very real to the American people in the late twentieth century, and the attacks on September 11, 2001, fostered the War on Terror that has defined the new millennium thus far.

CHAPTER 1

THE 1960s

DURING A TURBULENT DECADE, AMERICA WOULD, UPON DISCOVERING Russian missile bases in Cuba, draw near to the brink of war with the Soviet Union, before becoming ever more deeply embroiled in a costly, increasingly unpopular and—for the first time—televised war fighting communism in Vietnam.

In 1959, the dictatorship of US-backed Fulgencio Batista in Cuba was overthrown by revolutionary forces led by Fidel Castro. Although Castro was not originally a Marxist, his land reforms threatened American commercial interests on the island, and he would go on to link himself with, and take aid from, the Soviet Union. Within a few years, America's greatest Cold War enemy not only had an ally less than 100 miles (160 kilometers) from Florida, but was building military bases on Cuba, too. The US had to wonder: would other, larger, Latin American countries now fall to communism?

Consequently in January 1961, the US broke off diplomatic relations with Cuba, and the CIA began drawing up plans to depose the new leader by way of an invasion of the island by anti-Castro exiles. Newly elected president John F. Kennedy was, however, unwilling to risk America being regarded as an imperialist power and stripped the mission of any overt

US involvement. Without air support, the operation was crippled; when it was launched in April, all 1,400 Cuban exiles were captured or killed on the beaches of Cuba's Bay of Pigs.

A week earlier, the US had suffered another embarrassment when the Soviet Union had dented America's pride once again, when it became the first nation to put a man in space. In response, Kennedy announced that America would put a man on the moon before the end of the decade.

Emboldened by success in space and the US failure at the Bay of Pigs, as well as America's lack of reaction when Soviet-controlled East Germany had built a wall across Berlin to stop East Germans leaving for the West, Soviet premier Nikita Khrushchev chose to strengthen his position in the Caribbean.

During the summer of 1962, the CIA noted the buildup of Soviet troops and equipment in Cuba, but it was not until October 16 that spy planes spotted evidence of Soviet medium-range nuclear missile bases on the island. Kennedy was advised by his joint chiefs of staff to launch a full military invasion of Cuba, but the president chose a more cautious path, announcing a blockade of the island.

Initially, Soviet ships en route to Cuba showed no signs of recognizing the blockade, and when a Russian submarine was seen supporting them, a US destroyer moved into position to engage the vessels. Was a world war about to break out? The world held its breath. Then, the Soviet ships stopped…and turned back. "We're eyeball to eyeball," said Secretary of State Dean Rush, "and I think the other guy just blinked." An immediate conflagration had been averted, but there were still Soviet missiles in Cuba directed at the United States. Anxiously, the world watched and waited. As the US began making plans for air strikes and a possible invasion, on October 27, only eleven days after the missiles had been spotted, an American U-2 spy plane was shot down over Cuba, killing its pilot.

Were nuclear missiles about to be launched? Who would be the first to blink this time? Again it was Khrushchev, who had a much smaller nuclear

The funeral of President John F. Kennedy on November 25, 1963. His widow, Jackie Kennedy, leads their children down the White House steps while, following on the left, is JFK's brother Attorney General Robert F. Kennedy, who himself would be assassinated five years later.

arsenal. Proposing that he and Kennedy show "statesmanlike wisdom," the Soviet leader withdrew his missiles on the agreement that the US wouldn't invade Cuba. Khrushchev also asked that America remove its nuclear missiles from Turkey, which Kennedy refused to do publicly—while secretly acquiescing.

WERE NUCLEAR MISSILES ABOUT TO BE LAUNCHED? WHO WOULD BE THE FIRST TO BLINK THIS TIME?

A group of Cuban soldiers after routing the invasion by exiles at the Bay of Pigs in 1961. Stripped of any overt US backing in the form of air support, the invasion had been a fiasco.

The Cuban missile crisis was as close as the superpowers came to nuclear war. The following summer, they made a step towards détente, signing a treaty banning nuclear tests in the atmosphere. US conflict with communist regimes would, however, continue, but not directly against the Soviet Union. Instead, America would fight both overtly and covertly, and most bloodily in southeast Asia.

VIETNAM AND THE DOMINO THEORY

Like Germany after World War II and Korea in 1950, Vietnam was in 1956 divided into two parts: a communist North and a capitalist South. The country had been part of the French colony of Indochina since the late nineteenth century, when, in the 1940s, a nationalist movement, the Viet Minh, led by Ho Chi Minh, began to emerge. From the early 1950s, the Viet Minh had received support from the new communist government in China, and, through insurrections in the north of Vietnam, had eroded France's desire to keep its colony.

Kennedy addresses the nation during the Cuban Missile Crisis in 1962, stating that America would "regard any nuclear missile launched from Cuba against any nation in the western hemisphere as an attack by the Soviet Union on the United States."

After the defeat of their garrison at Dien Bien Phu in 1954, the French gave up, and, as the French withdrew, Vietnam was partitioned, albeit initially on a "temporary" basis, at the Geneva Conference of 1956. President Eisenhower and others, however, were worried that if the whole of Vietnam fell into communist hands, the rest of southeast Asia would follow, like "a row of dominoes." That would then pose a threat to Australasia.

Elections were supposed to be held in Vietnam in 1956 to decide on a new government across a unified country. But, fearing that Ho Chi Minh's communists might win, Eisenhower blocked them, backing instead a separate South Vietnam state, and propping it up with $1 billion of economic aid and military assistance. Its leader, Ngo Dinh Diem, was anti-communist, anti-French and a Catholic in a largely Buddhist country, and in a rule that harked back to colonial ways, he prevented land reforms, and relied on the landed elite and his relatives to maintain power. By the end of the 1950s, a communist guerrilla movement in the South backed by North Vietnam and called the Viet Cong (Vietnamese Communists) had been formed. In response, in late 1961, President Kennedy increased American aid and "military advisers" to help bolster the South. When Kennedy came into office in 1961, there were 2,000 American troops in Vietnam; by the end of 1963, there were 16,000. This escalating trend would continue throughout the decade.

What had largely been a covert war became front-page news when attacks on Buddhists by Diem provoked large protests. Photographs of monks sitting in flames as, having poured petrol over their gowns, they set fire to themselves, went around the world. Reluctantly, Kennedy accepted the advice of aides that the US should, for the sake of stability in South Vietnam, support a military coup against Diem. On November 1, 1963, the generals toppled Diem, later shooting him and his brother. Kennedy ordered a review of his options in Vietnam, including the possibility of US withdrawal, but he never read the report. Before the end of the month he, too, was dead.

Buddhist monk Thich Quang Duc sets himself on fire in Saigon in June 1963, in protest at the persecution of Buddhists by the US-backed South Vietnamese government. In the following months, five more Buddhist monks would kill themselves in the same way.

JFK'S ASSASSINATION

Riding in a motorcade in Dallas, Texas, on November 22, 1963, President Kennedy was shot, dying on the way to hospital. But more than half a century later, who—and on whose orders—delivered the fatal shot, remains a question still pondered by many. The Warren Commission investigation into the shooting reported in September 1964 that three rifle shots were fired by a lone gunman from the Texas School Book Depository building as the motorcade passed. That lone gunman was 24-year-old Lee Harvey Oswald, a former US Marines marksman who had defected to the Soviet Union in the late 1950s, before returning to Texas. He had begun working at the book depository the previous month.

With a witness description of a sniper firing from the building, Oswald was soon challenged on a street by a policeman. Pulling out a revolver, Oswald shot the policeman dead, before fleeing into a cinema,

The assassination of John F. Kennedy in Dallas, Texas, on November 22, 1963. In the back of the car, Jackie Kennedy leans over the wounded president before the fatal, final shot hits.

where he was arrested. Two days later, Oswald was being led through Dallas Police Headquarters when Jack Ruby, a local nightclub operator, stepped out of the crowd and shot him. Within two hours, Oswald himself was dead, while Ruby would die in prison four years later awaiting retrial over his murder charge.

Although the Warren Commission found that both Oswald (and Ruby) had been acting alone, other witnesses said that the second and third shots—the third being the fatal one to Kennedy's head—didn't come from the book depository. Was there a conspiracy? Certainly for many people it was too shocking to accept that one unstable young man with a rifle could kill the president.

Skepticism about the assassination among the general public and even on Capitol Hill was still strong enough that in 1976 a House Select Committee on Assassinations (HSCA) was established. It concluded that JFK was probably assassinated as part of a conspiracy. It didn't suggest who the conspirators might be, though it ruled out many suspects, such as the governments of the Soviet Union and Cuba, as well as the Mafia, FBI, CIA, and Secret Service. Would any part of the US security services seriously have wanted Kennedy dead? There was the suggestion that he was regarded by some right-wing zealots as having gone soft on communism as he had promised not to invade Cuba, had looked as if he might withdraw from Vietnam, and had sympathized with the Civil Rights Movement, which some regarded as communist subversion. The HSCA also reported that the security services had withheld information from the Warren Commission. Was there a sinister reason for this or was it just secretive agencies being true to their nature, and giving away as little as possible? Or was the fatal shot a terrible error that the Secret Service then hushed up? One theory suggests that in the commotion after Oswald's first shot, a Secret Service agent in the car behind the president's accidentally fired his weapon, killing JFK.

Whether conspiracy, human error, or the efforts of a lone, deranged gunman, Kennedy's assassination stunned the world. The presidency, though, had to continue. Two hours after the shooting, Vice President Lyndon B. Johnson, who had been in the motorcade that day, was sworn in as president on Air Force One as the plane prepared to leave Dallas.

IT CONCLUDED THAT JFK WAS PROBABLY ASSASSINATED AS PART OF A CONSPIRACY.

Two hours after the Kennedy assassination, Vice President Lyndon B. Johnson is sworn in as president on board Air Force One. Jackie Kennedy stands beside him.

US aircraft bomb a military target in North Vietnam in June 1966. Although the bombing of North Vietnam caused immense damage, it had little long-term effect on the war, as factories were simply rebuilt in the countryside.

VIET CONG GAINS

The coup against Diem had not improved the situation in South Vietnam. Instead, it had led to instability, with six governments coming and going in the following 18 months. Meanwhile, the Viet Cong gained effective control of half of the South, with North Vietnamese Army units pressing southwards. It was becoming ever more difficult, and, unlike in the Korean War, America—though supported by the South Vietnamese Army, South Korea, Australia, and New Zealand—didn't have the peace-keeping banner of a United Nations flag to help maintain popular support.

Advisers to President Johnson ranged from a few "doves" who advocated cutting their losses and pulling out of Vietnam, to a majority of "hawks," who felt that they could not allow South Vietnam to fail because America had already invested so much in the conflict.

Efforts to save the South escalated. Following the killing of eight Americans at the US base at Pleiku in February 1965, bombing against North Vietnam began and the number of US troops in Vietnam increased vastly. Johnson, for his part, tried to dodge his exposure to any potential political and public disapproval by not seeking full congressional support, instead relying on a resolution from August 1964 that authorized him to take "all necessary measures" against armed attack on US forces. Nor did he ask Congress to increase taxes to fund the war, instead increasing government borrowing.

THE GUERRILLA ADVANTAGE

By the end of 1967, nearly half a million US troops were in Vietnam and 16,000 had died. The bombing of North Vietnam caused great damage, but had little effect on the course of the war, as factories were simply rebuilt in the countryside, and supply lines established through the jungle and Cambodia to support the Viet Cong in the South. As James

Thomson of the National Security Council remarked, the North Vietnamese knew very well that "someday we're going to go home." It was a classic guerrilla war situation: the Viet Cong, backed by the North Vietnamese Army (NVA), could win by holding out; America could only win by achieving total victory.

BY THE END OF 1967, NEARLY HALF A MILLION US TROOPS WERE IN VIETNAM AND 16,000 HAD DIED.

Yes, America had tanks, helicopters, and airplanes, but these all cost it the element of surprise. Between 1966 and 1968, the CIA noted that less than one percent of nearly two million Allied small unit operations resulted in enemy contact. They were losing many casualties to an enemy they often couldn't find. In contrast, in the same period, three-quarters of the battles were fought at the Viet Cong's choosing of time and place. One method to flush out the enemy was to drop defoliating chemicals, such as Agent Orange, to destroy forests and fields. Between 1962 and 1971, the US sprayed 20 million gallons (76 million liters) of defoliants on Vietnam, Laos, and parts of Cambodia. The severity of the long-term health and ecological consequences of this are still being hotly debated. Furthermore, the Viet Cong were being supplied by North Vietnam, but North Vietnam was itself being supplied by China and the Soviet Union. America, however, wasn't going to bomb *those* supply lines, as that would antagonize the communist heavyweights.

THE TET OFFENSIVE

On January 30, 1968, during a temporary truce for Vietnam's New Year holiday of Tet, the NVA and the Viet Cong launched major assaults on cities and towns all over the South. It was an immense shock for the US, and a further blow against support for the war when it was reported on American television news each evening.

Saigon under attack from the Viet Cong and North Vietnamese Army during the 1968 Tet Offensive. Having caught the US forces completely by surprise, the Tet Offensive was a great propaganda victory for the communists.

Although in terms of propaganda the Tet Offensive was a victory for the Viet Cong, it turned into a military defeat. Within a few weeks, the US had responded, killing or wounding most of the Viet Cong leadership. From then on, America's main enemy was the NVA, but with both sides digging in, the war was reaching a stalemate. In March, Johnson addressed the nation. Saying that bombing would cease and that peace negotiations were being opened, he indicated how unpopular the war had made him by announcing that he would not be standing for a second term.

MY LAI MASSACRE

In the efforts to regain dominance after the Tet Offensive, US military intelligence suspected that the My Lai settlements in Quảng Ngãi Province were harboring members of the Viet Cong. A search-and-destroy mission was planned, with the orders from Colonel Oran K. Henderson, the 11th Infantry Brigade commander, being to "go in there aggressively, close with the enemy and wipe them out for good." In turn, Captain Ernest Medina told his troops that the genuine villagers would have left for market, so any remaining people would be Viet Cong members or their supporters, who should be shot. Opinions differ on Medina's exact orders, but some, including platoon leaders, later claimed that they were told to kill "suspects," including women and children.

On March 16, around 100 soldiers, led by Captain Medina, landed in helicopters at My Lai. With Medina's command post remaining outside the villages, the 1st Platoon, led by Second Lieutenant William Calley Jr., entered the hamlet of Tu Cung. Although they met no resistance from villagers, the troops soon began firing indiscriminately at them. "They were shooting women and children…," remembered Private Michael Bernhardt, who refused to shoot anyone. A number of women and girls were gang-raped. The 2nd Platoon also killed more than 70 people, while seven of its men were wounded by mines and booby traps.

Flying overhead, helicopter pilot Hugh Thompson Jr. landed and intervened, telling American soldiers that if they shot any more villagers he would shoot them in return. He rescued at least 12 villagers and saw them on to helicopters, before reporting the incident, which led to the operation being called off.

"I don't remember seeing one military-age male in the entire place, dead or alive," Private Bernhardt would later say, but Lieutenant Calley reported a body count of 90 Viet Cong, with no civilians dead. Fighting a guerrilla war, body count rather than territorial gain was valued by the US military, and some officers were willing to accept dead civilians as Viet Cong to boost their body count numbers. As the Viet Cong was a guerrilla army drawn from civilians, the distinction between the two was, at times, blurred. Despite Thompson's report, it was decided that there was no basis for an investigation. A year passed before Ronald L. Ridenhour, a door gunner who had not been at My Lai but had heard about the massacre from some of those present, compiled statements from witnesses. Returning home after completing his tour of duty, he sent the evidence to 30 members of Congress. Three took up his plea to look into the incident. With word spreading, that November—18 months after the massacre—journalist Seymour Hersh's story of My Lai was published through the Associated Press wire service. Trials began the following November, at which Lieutenant Calley claimed that he was following orders from Captain Medina. Medina, in turn, denied giving the order to kill civilians and was acquitted. Convicted for the premeditated murder of 22 civilians, Calley's life sentence was reduced to 20 years on appeal; he eventually served three and a half years under house arrest. Charges were brought against 12 other men, but none was found guilty, though five were court-martialed and others demoted. In contrast, 30 years after My Lai, Hugh Thompson and his fellow helicopter crewmen were awarded the Soldier's Medal for their actions in saving Vietnamese lives that day.

To some extent, My Lai can be seen as a crisis of discipline and morale among the forces in a controversial war that was costing many American lives while showing no signs of long-term victory. It may have been the bloodiest massacre in the conflict—the US estimate is 347 dead and the Vietnamese figure is 504, with ages ranging from one to 80—but other soldiers later reported that there had been "a My Lai each month for over a year" during 1968–1969.

The massacre by a US Army platoon of between 347 and 504 unarmed Vietnamese men, women, and children in the My Lai settlements in 1968 was one of the darkest episodes of the war for America.

THE SIEGE OF KHE SANH

An important outpost in the northwestern mountains of South Vietnam, the Khe Sanh Combat Base was just 14 miles (23 km) south of the Demilitarized Zone that separated North and South Vietnam and 7 miles (11 km) from the border with Laos.

By early 1968, North Vietnamese troops had succeeded in encircling the base, cutting it off by land and pounding it daily with artillery. What followed was one of the longest, bloodiest battles in the war. For five months, supplies and reinforcements were flown in to the base, while a massive American aerial bombardment was launched, dropping more than 100,000 tons of bombs on the surrounding area.

While the effectiveness and ethics of high-altitude B-52 bombers dropping 65-ton bombs on patches of jungle was debatable, psychologically they were crucial. "When the Marines see the piles of smoke rising across the valley," wrote English journalist David Leitch, reporting for the *Sunday Times* from inside Khe Sanh in February 1968, "they feel that someone is remembering them."

But bombs were not the only weapon. To keep the North Vietnamese Army at bay, in the first four weeks of the siege, 60,000 tons of the incendiary weapon, napalm, were dropped on the area surrounding the base, setting the jungle on fire. The siege ended when a relief operation broke through to the Marines. But with the base finally liberated, the new American commander in Vietnam, General Creighton Abrams, decided to evacuate Khe Sanh for good, deeming it too risky to maintain such a vulnerable position. With the Americans gone, on July 9, the North Vietnamese flag was raised at the base.

In all, almost 3,000 US and South Vietnamese soldiers were killed in the siege and relief operation, with more than 9,000 wounded, while the NVA saw more than 2,500 killed in action. It was the first US combat base to be abandoned due to enemy pressure.

Besieged and bombarded for five months in 1968, the Marines at Khe Sanh were finally rescued and the combat base abandoned.

FLASHPOINT IN CHICAGO

Before Lyndon Johnson left office, the Vietnam War would provoke scenes of violence in America. Following anti-war college campus demonstrations and sit-ins, physical encounters with the police became more common, as did active draft resistance and the destruction of draft cards. And when anti-war protesters converged outside the Democratic Nation Convention in Chicago that August, the mayor sent out 12,000

Protesters surround a police car at the Democratic National Convention in Chicago in August 1968. An increasingly unpopular conflict at home, the war in Vietnam provoked many mass demonstrations across the United States.

THE ASSASSINATION OF ROBERT F. KENNEDY

Having been Attorney General while his brother John F. Kennedy was president, by the summer of 1968, Robert F. Kennedy was a senator running as a Democrat candidate in the primaries for the presidential election. Following an address to his campaign supporters at the Ambassador Hotel, Los Angeles, on June 5, Kennedy was being led out through the kitchen when he was shot by 24-year-old Sirhan Sirhan. The following day, Kennedy died from his wounds.

HIS PRESIDENCY WOULD NOW VIRTUALLY BE BOOKENDED BY THE ASSASSINATIONS OF TWO KENNEDY BROTHERS.

Sirhan, a Jordanian citizen from a Palestinian Christian family, had moved to America when he was 12. In recent months, he had become fixated on assassinating Kennedy after the senator pledged to send fighter jets to support the state of Israel. Easily apprehended after the shooting, Sirhan was sentenced to death, but this was commuted to life when California abolished the death penalty in 1972. Coming just two months after Martin Luther King Jr.'s assassination, Johnson called for tougher gun laws, but he had said the same after JFK's death to no effect. His presidency would now virtually be bookended by the assassinations of two Kennedy brothers.

armed police, supported by the Illinois National Guard to confront them. Caught by TV news cameras were scenes of armed forces clubbing not just the marginalized or suppressed, as might have happened earlier in the Civil Rights Movement, but many white, middle-class, well-educated Americans. The violence divided the nation. Abe Ribicoff, Democratic senator for Connecticut, deplored the "Gestapo tactics" of the police, but Hubert Humphrey, who would become the Democratic candidate in the election, dismissed the demonstrators as people who "feel that all they have to do is riot and they'll get their way."

The clashes in Chicago did not discourage protests. The following year, millions across America—united across age, race, and economic differences—demonstrated against the war in the Vietnam Moratorium.

THE MANSON MURDERS

When followers joined Charles Manson's so-called Family, they may have thought they had found the guru to give meaning to their lives. In fact, they had entered what would turn into a murderous cult. In 1968, Charles Manson, having spent more than half his life in and out of young offenders' institutions and prisons, had recently managed to tap into the Californian hippie scene. The slight, good-looking 34-year-old's ambition was to become a singer-songwriter, and one of his songs even appeared as a Beach Boys B-side after he had temporarily befriended one of the group. His real talent, however, turned out to be the manipulation of unstable young minds, and soon he was collecting drug users and dropouts in San Francisco and Los Angeles.

Prophesying a black–white race war based on his insane interpretation of the Book of Revelation and a nonsensical reading of the Beatles' 1968 song "Helter Skelter," Manson had a dark charisma so mesmerizing that at its height his Family had 35 members. Such was his control of the Family that he didn't even need to lead them into carnage. Instead, he sent others to do his bidding. It was Family member Tex Watson who broke into film director Roman Polanski's house in Benedict Canyon, Los Angeles, on August 8, 1969. Polanski was away, but his wife, model and actress Sharon Tate, was at home with three friends. Watson was accompanied by Susan Atkins and Patricia Krenwinkel. Outside, Linda Kasabian was their driver, and Manson remained at the Family's ranch. What followed were fatal stabbings and shootings of a heavily pregnant Tate and her friends Abigail Folger, Voytek Frykowski, and celebrity hairdresser Jay Sebring. Each was stabbed multiple times, while a passerby, Steven Parent, was shot dead.

Charles Manson in court in June 1970. The following month he carved an X into his forehead. Susan Atkins, Patricia Krenwinkel, and Leslie Van Houten soon copied him.

It was a crime that shocked and frightened not only Hollywood, but the entire United States and beyond. In a decade that had seen much racial violence, war, and brutal altercations at demonstrations, the frenzy that Manson had generated seemed to be utterly without motive. The house where Polanski and Sharon Tate were living was known to Manson, as it had formerly been occupied by Terry Melcher, the record producer son of singer Doris Day and friend of the Beach Boys. But there seems to be no reason why Tate and her friends were targeted, or why the following day Manson and 10 of his family murdered a supermarket executive, Leno LaBianca, and his wife Rosemary, a dress shop co-owner. The LaBiancas were completely unknown to Manson. With two further deaths of people in Manson's sphere, a total of nine murders were committed by the Family over a five-week period.

Even when Manson and the other suspects were arrested, his sinister hold over the Family continued. Those on trial often acted in chilling unity in the courtroom, while other members of the cult uninvolved in the killings failed to disband despite their leader's absence.

With Linda Kasabian—who had not participated in the killings themselves—acting as a prosecution witness, Manson and the rest received death sentences. However, these were later commuted to life sentences.

DEATHS AT ALTAMONT

Four months after the Manson murders, the world of 1960s' pop music would be sullied by a violent death. Having drawn criticism on their 1969 US tour for charging high ticket prices, The Rolling Stones announced that the tour's final concert on December 6, 1969 would be free. But the concert, held after a last-minute change of venue at the Altamont Speedway in San Joaquin County, California, was ill-prepared, with a low stage leaving the bands vulnerable to the audience rushing them.

Having provided security for other bands, a group of Hells Angels was asked to keep the stage clear of crowd members. In return, although some dispute this, it is said that they were paid $500 in beer—which they could drink throughout the day-long festival.

During the course of the day, the mood at the concert was fractious, with some of the 300,000-strong crowd fighting each other, as well as

Manson Family members Susan Atkins, Patricia Krenwinkel, and Leslie Van Houten arrive in court in June 1970. Van Houten wasn't involved in the killings at Sharon Tate's house but admitted her part in murdering Leno and Rosemary LaBianca.

the Hells Angels, and even throwing bottles at the performers. The behavior of the Hells Angels, some now drunk, also deteriorated. While performing, Marty Balin of Jefferson Airplane was knocked unconscious by an Angel.

The violence reached its peak when, during The Rolling Stones' set, 18-year-old Meredith Hunter, high on amphetamines, tried to climb onto the stage. Following a scuffle with Hells Angels, he was pushed back into the crowd, before reemerging with a revolver. Seeing this, Hells Angel Alan Passaro pulled out a knife and stabbed Hunter twice, killing him. On the stage, The Rolling Stones were aware of the commotion, but not its severity, and played on. Pleading self-defense, Passaro

Audience members look on as Hells Angels beat a fan with pool cues at the Rolling Stones' Altamont Free Concert in California in December 1969. By the end of the one-day festival, four people were dead.

was acquitted of murder, but Hunter's death was not the only fatality at the festival. Two people were killed in a hit-and-run, and another drowned in a drainage ditch. In addition, there were numerous thefts. In contrast with the "peace and love" atmosphere at the Woodstock Festival in New York state four months earlier, Altamont was a sour end to a decade that had seen such a burst of creativity in rock and roll.

NIXON IN THE WHITE HOUSE

By the time Republican Richard Nixon entered the White House in January 1969, the US presence was at its height in Vietnam, with 543,000 military personnel in the country. Although Nixon was determined to

The inauguration of President Richard Nixon in January 1969. Nixon was determined to end the war in Vietnam, but it would take longer than he hoped, and he would no longer be in office when the end finally came.

end the war, the heaviest bombing came in his first few months, and peace talks were still in deadlock when Ho Chi Minh died that September.

There was, however, some positive news for America: having been beaten into space by the Soviet Union and having suffered a disaster when a fire during a test at Cape Kennedy caused the deaths of three astronauts, in July 1969 the Apollo 11 mission fulfilled Kennedy's pledge to put a man on the Moon before the end of the decade. The 1960s ended with 200 Americans still dying each week in Vietnam, while the US looked for a way to withdraw from the conflict without losing face. Meanwhile, at home, anti-war protests were becoming more radical and violent. If the decade drew to a close with a public sense of disenchantment with the government, things would become even worse over the next few years.

THE 1960S ENDED WITH 200 AMERICANS STILL DYING EACH WEEK IN VIETNAM.

CHAPTER 2

DISCONTENT AND REVIVAL

IN THE 1970S, RICHARD NIXON SUCCEEDED IN FINALLY DISENTANGLING America from Vietnam, but his underhanded methods of government would lead to his downfall—while also revealing a sinister culture of espionage within the United States.

For his own protection, President Nixon was ushered, in May 1970, from the White House to his retreat at Camp David, 62 miles (100 km) outside Washington, DC. America wasn't under attack from a foreign power, but from some of its own people, as a crowd of 100,000 protesters amassed in the capital, some smashing windows and dragging parked cars to use as road blocks.

They had been provoked by the shooting of students by the Ohio National Guard at Kent State University earlier that month. The students, reacting to news that the war in Vietnam was being expanded to target Viet Cong forces in Cambodia, had been demonstrating for four days and had set fire to the college's officer training corps building. Although some students were still throwing stones, the main demonstration was

A demonstrator at the University of California, Berkeley, throws a tear gas canister at police in May 1970. Anti-Vietnam War protests intensified across America after the US invasion of Cambodia in April 1970.

largely dispersing, when at least 29 of the 77 guardsmen fired on the crowd. In all, four students were killed—two of whom had been walking between classes and were uninvolved in the demonstration. Another nine were injured.

It remains unclear why the guardsmen fired when no order had been given. Some of them later claimed that they had been fired upon, although this has never been established, and the crowd posed little physical threat—the closest person hit by the guardsmen's bullets was 71 feet (22 meters) away. A President's Commission found the guardsmen's actions unjustified and eight were indicted by a grand jury. The

Protesting students at Kent State University in Ohio in May 1970 flee after tear gas is fired by the National Guard. After four days of demonstrations, National Guardsman opened fire on the protesters, killing four students and injuring nine others.

charges, however, were dismissed on the grounds that they were too weak to warrant a trial. Other protests were sparked by the shootings. Four days later, 11 people at the University of New Mexico were attacked by the National Guard armed with bayonets; the next week, police and state highway patrolmen killed two students and wounded nine others at the all-black Jackson State University in Mississippi. In all, 450 colleges across America closed following both violent and nonviolent protests. "This is not the greatest free democracy in the world," remarked Charles Colson, counsel to Richard Nixon, on seeing the 82nd Airborne Division brought in to Washington to restore order. "This is a nation at war with itself."

Five days after the Kent State shootings, 100,000 people gathered in Washington, DC, in protest. Upon seeing the carnage and the military presence, Charles Colson, counsel to Richard Nixon, remarked, "This is a nation at war with itself."

ATTICA PRISON RIOT

In September the following year, 2,200 prisoners at Attica Correctional Facility in New York state rioted, taking 42 staff hostage. The prison chapel was burned down and guards were beaten, with one thrown out of a window. He later died from his injuries.

Railing against overcrowding and the brutality of the prison guards, the prisoners drew up a list of 27 demands. Although New York Correction Commissioner Russell Oswald agreed to improve conditions for the prisoners, negotiations broke down over the rioters' call for an amnesty from prosecution for their rioting. Four days of talks had ended in deadlock when tear gas was dropped into the prison, before New York State Police troopers fired into the smoke, killing 25 inmates and 10 hostages.

FOUR DAYS OF TALKS HAD ENDED IN DEADLOCK WHEN TEAR GAS WAS DROPPED INTO THE PRISON.

Attica State Prison shortly after New York State Police troopers ended the four-day riot and siege in 1971. When the uprising was over, 43 people were dead, including 10 prison officers and civilian staff and 33 inmates.

With an investigation launched into the handling of the siege, the New York State Special Commission reported that, with the exception of Indian massacres in the late nineteenth century, the State Police assault "was the bloodiest one-day encounter between Americans since the Civil War."

NIXON IN CHINA

Determined to extricate America from the war in Vietnam without losing face, Nixon calculated that a thaw in relations with China would help detach it from North Vietnam and make US negotiations with Hanoi easier. It would also, he hoped, exploit a recent split between China and the Soviet Union. Following a secret mission by national security adviser Henry Kissinger to Beijing in 1971, Nixon flew to China the following February to begin normalizing relations between the two countries.

His calculation proved correct. The Soviet Union, fearing being isolated if China and America became too close, softened its stance towards the US, and that summer the president went to Moscow to agree to a deal on arms control. Nixon's achievement was welcomed as a step towards ending the Cold War, but he had only managed this success by bypassing Congress, bureaucracy, and the media. Such methods would prove to be the president's undoing.

In Vietnam, US troop numbers had already been reduced, but periodic heavy bombing continued during negotiations. Then, in January 1973, Nixon announced that a ceasefire to end the war had been agreed upon. American forces would pull out and POWs were to be returned, with South Vietnam guaranteed the right to determine its own political future. That was a guarantee only in theory: Nixon had failed to mention that North Vietnamese troops had been allowed to remain in the South.

THE CLIMATE OF SECRECY AND PARANOIA THAT NIXON HAD CULTIVATED WAS TO BLAME.

President Richard Nixon and Chinese Premier Zhou Enlai normalize relations between the two countries in February 1972. Nixon was the first US president to visit the People's Republic of China, which was established in 1949.

THE CHILEAN COUP

How long do state visits last? A few days? Perhaps a week. In late 1971, Cuban Prime Minister Fidel Castro made a state visit to Chile that lasted a month. Castro was the guest of Marxist President Salvador Allende, who, since his election the previous year, had begun nationalizing industries, including US-owned copper mines. Fearing a government like that of Cuba emerging in South America, the Nixon administration had already authorized $10 million for the CIA to support opposition to

General Augusto Pinochet is flanked by the heads of the Chilean Navy and Air Force after his successful military coup in Chile in 1973. The CIA had secretly spent millions of dollars helping put Pinochet into power.

Allende. In addition, America hampered Allende's economic development plans by persuading the World Bank to cease any loans to Chile. Then, on September 11, 1973, the Chilean military attacked the government, with fighter jets firing into the presidential palace. Refusing to surrender, Allende shot himself.

The US promptly recognized the new military junta led by the Commander-in-Chief of Chile's armed forces, General Augusto Pinochet Ugarte. Pinochet's free-market politics may have suited American commercial interests, but his brutal regime involved the kidnapping and murder of more than 3,000 political opponents, including two Americans.

It would not be until 1990 that, after much pressure, Pinochet would relinquish power. Later arrested for human rights violations, he died while awaiting trial in 2006.

WATERGATE

In the 1968 election, Nixon had only just scraped into the White House, but in 1972 he won a landslide victory. Yet, within two years he would be forced to resign.

Although it would have seemed ridiculous to suggest so at the time, Nixon's presidency began to unravel on the night of June 17, 1972, when five men were arrested breaking into, and attempting to bug, the Democratic National Committee in the Watergate apartment complex in Washington.

One of the men was said to be a former CIA employee, and an investigation led by *Washington Post* reporters Bob Woodward and Carl Bernstein, and aided by secret tips from the FBI's Associate Director Mark Felt, managed to link the burglars to payments from the Committee to reelect the President. Nixon denied any White House involvement in the burglary—and, to be fair, he probably didn't know about it in advance. But the climate of secrecy and paranoia that he had cultivated was to blame. He had sanctioned break-ins and wire-taps of opponents, and the arrested burglars did have ties to the White House, as well as to an underworld of CIA agents and anti-Castro Cuban activists.

Personally, Nixon had set up a special intelligence operation of "plumbers" to plug government leaks, such as the Pentagon Papers, which revealed that American bombing in southeast Asia under President Johnson had reached into Laos and Cambodia. Similarly, Nixon's dirty tricks targeted Democratic candidates running in 1972. To give one example, they destabilized Democratic Senator Edmund Muskie's efforts by forging a letter to a New Hampshire newspaper, claiming that Muskie had made disparaging remarks about French-Canadians. With stronger

With his family beside him, Richard Nixon resigns in August 1974. Perhaps beginning to understand the nature of his downfall, Nixon bade farewell to his White House staff by saying, "Those who hate you don't win unless you hate them, and then you destroy yourself."

White House counsel John Dean had organized the cover-up following the Watergate break-in. But, with the investigation claiming ever more senior White House figures, in April 1973 he agreed to testify before the Senate committee.

contenders displaced, ultimately the Democrat party fielded George McGovern, one of its weaker candidates, and Nixon won a firm victory. More broadly, Nixon's methods were characteristic of the time. In response to anti-war protests, the secret services and law enforcement agencies had, since the mid-1960s and without legal authority, bugged and kept leftist movements under electronic surveillance. Specifically, the FBI's Counter Intelligence Program, COINTELPRO, was established to target civil rights organizations.

THE END FOR NIXON

While Nixon was providing hush money to keep the Watergate burglars and their associates quiet, a Democrat-dominated Senate established a committee to investigate the whole matter. The more questions that were asked, the higher the trail led—right up to the White House. Under questioning, one aide revealed that Nixon taped his White House conversations. Although earlier presidents had recorded some of their conversations, Nixon had taped more than 3,000 hours. After some obstructions, the president was forced to hand over the tapes, evidence from which allowed a case for impeachment to begin.

With the release of a transcript that revealed Nixon attempting to stop the FBI's investigation into Watergate, his fate was sealed. Republican support in Congress fell away and, with impeachment looming, Nixon

President Ronald Reagan announcing the Strategic Defense Initiative (SDI) in 1983. Commonly known as the Star Wars project, this system would, if it worked, intercept enemy nuclear missiles and destroy them.

resigned on August 9, 1974. He is the only American president to have done so. Watergate had brought Nixon down, but the affair was a testament to American democracy. Nixon's shady dealings had surfaced and justice had prevailed. Furthermore, a number of his White House staff served prison terms. Between 1974 and 1976, presidential and congressional committees investigated the misdeeds of the intelligence community, exposing the FBI's COINTELPRO and fueling a broader suspicion among the American people of the federal government and law enforcement.

THE END IN VIETNAM

Nixon had been able in 1973 to withdraw US ground troops, while continuing the bombing campaign to support an independent South Vietnam. But the South was a fragile, corrupt state where, two years later, inflation was at 65 percent and soldiers were deserting the army. In March 1975, the North Vietnamese Army suddenly pushed through the South and the following month all of Vietnam and Cambodia fell to communists. In the final days, a mob gathered at the US embassy in Saigon as people tried to catch the final places on the helicopters that were airlifting Americans and refugees to warships in the South China Sea. On April 30, the last US helicopter left, just hours before NVA tanks bulldozed the gates of the presidential palace. Thus ended America's 15-year involvement in Vietnam.

Financially, and in terms of casualties, the war had been a hugely costly failure for America. It had claimed 58,000 American lives and an estimated two million Vietnamese. In addition, the US had dropped a greater tonnage of bombs on Vietnam than it had on Germany, Italy, and Japan combined during World War II, causing not just destruction, but long-term ecological damage. Since 2000, US Congress has allocated more than $84 million in operations to

THE WAR HAD CLAIMED 58,000 AMERICAN LIVES AND AN ESTIMATED TWO MILLION VIETNAMESE.

THE JONESTOWN MASSACRE

Leo Ryan's final days began in November 1978 when, as chairman of a congressional subcommittee with jurisdiction over US citizens living abroad, he flew to Guyana in Latin America to investigate Jim Jones's Peoples Temple cult.

Having claimed holy powers from an early age, Jones had set up the Peoples Temple in Indianapolis in 1956. Emphasizing racial integrity, in its early years the church's mix of Christianity and socialism did some good work in the community, such as organizing soup kitchens. Nine years later, the Temple moved to California. But Jones was a con man: he used spies to steal information that he could use to foster his claim to be clairvoyant, and stooges would fake being wheelchair-bound before he "healed" them. He was also excellent at controlling people and at raising money. By 1975, the Temple's assets were estimated to be $10 million. Of course, members had to offer up everything they had to Jones—their possessions, their children, and their bodies. When accusations began to surface of the misappropriation of funds, Jones sought a new home for the Temple, and bought remote land in the Guyanese jungle. In May 1977, 1,000 members of the Temple left California for their new life in Jonestown, Guyana. Described as an agricultural commune, Jonestown was, from the reports of those who escaped, more like a concentration camp, where members worked 11-hour shifts in the fields, camped in unsanitary conditions, were fed inadequate rations, and suffered a number of ailments. If they didn't work hard enough, they were subjected to public beatings by armed guards. Meanwhile, to keep the people suppressed and maintain Jones's claims that he was now God, telephone calls were forbidden, mail was censored, and passports and money were confiscated.

Leo Ryan was joined on his trip to Guyana by concerned relatives of cult members and some journalists. Reaching Jonestown in two small aircraft, Ryan's group spent two days talking to Temple members, before preparing to fly out with 14 members who wanted to leave the cult. The first departing aircraft was already taxiing down the runway when one of the supposed defectors on board, Larry Layton, opened fire on the passengers. With that, other members who had escorted the visiting party back to the planes began shooting, killing Ryan, three journalists, and a defecting Temple member, while wounding others. Survivors fled into the fields as other passengers managed to subdue Layton and radio for help.

When the Guyanese Army cut through the jungle into Jonestown the following day, they found 909 dead bodies, 260 of them children. The few who had hidden in the fields had survived, but almost all the

Peoples Temple members had either drunk, or been injected with, cyanide, while Jones himself had died of a gunshot wound to the head. Like a Pied Piper, Jones had led his followers into the wilderness. When his cult was threatened, Jones himself, it is assumed, brought about its destruction. Until the September 11 attacks in 2001, the Jonestown mass suicide was the largest single loss of American civilian life in a deliberate act.

There were 909 victims in the Jonestown massacre in Guyana, November 1978. Members of Jim Jones's Peoples Temple cult had either drunk or been injected with cyanide.

decontaminate Vietnamese land from the effects of Agent Orange and other chemical weapons.

After Vietnam, there were consequences on Capitol Hill, too. Following Johnson's and Nixon's waging of a war without ever making a formal declaration, in November 1973 the War Powers Act was passed. This prevented a president using US troops in combat for more than 60 days without congressional approval.

THE NEW COLD WAR

"Peace does not come from weakness or retreat. It comes from the restoration of American military superiority," declared Ronald Reagan in 1976, when he was challenging President Gerald Ford as the Republican candidate. Reagan didn't win that time, and Democrat Jimmy Carter replaced Ford in the White House. However, when Reagan did become president in 1981, his tone was markedly belligerent in contrast to that of Ford or Carter. Denouncing the Soviet Union as "the evil empire" in 1983, he announced the Strategic Defense Initiative (SDI). Commonly known as the "Star Wars" project, this system would, if it worked, intercept enemy nuclear missiles and destroy them.

Anti-communist Reagan was in fact strongly opposed to nuclear weapons. And with a new, relatively young, reforming Soviet leader, Mikhail Gorbachev, now in office, Reagan and his Soviet counterpart began a series of summits in Europe to discuss arms reductions. These meetings culminated, in December 1987, in a treaty on intermediate-range nuclear weapons. It was the first time that the superpowers had ever reduced their arsenals.

SPACE SHUTTLE DISASTERS

Beginning operational flights in 1982, NASA's five space shuttles flew 135 missions before being retired almost 30 years later. In that time, they suffered two disasters. In January 1986, the space shuttle *Challenger* fell apart 76 seconds into a flight, leading to the deaths of its seven crew members. Not designed to be used in such cold temperatures, a seal had failed on a rocket booster, causing an explosive fuel leak. Investigating the disaster, a commission found that NASA's organizational structure had led to warnings from engineers being ignored.

The space shuttle *Challenger* fell apart less than two minutes after launching in January 1986. A seal had failed on one of the rocket boosters, causing an explosive fuel leak. All seven astronauts on board were killed.

ASSASSINS

Less than three months into his presidency, Ronald Reagan was the victim of an assassination attempt. On March 30, 1981, 25-year-old John Hinckley Jr. was among the crowd outside the Hilton Hotel in Washington as Reagan left after addressing a conference. Just 15 ft. (4.6 m) from the president, Hinckley was able to fire six times at him, although only the final bullet hit Reagan. The president suffered a punctured lung but, rushed to hospital, the 70-year-old recovered well after surgery. Of the other shots, secret service agent Tim McCarthy was hit as he shielded the president, while police officer Thomas Delahanty and White House Press Secretary James Brady were also wounded. All survived the shooting, though Delahanty had to retire from the police and Brady was left partially paralyzed. Brady later successfully campaigned for stricter gun controls, with the Brady Act of 1993 making federal background checks on firearm purchases a requirement. Hinckley, meanwhile, having been found not guilty by reason of insanity, was detained under institutional psychiatric care until his release in 2016.

On December 8 the previous year, Mark Chapman had shot dead former Beatle John Lennon outside the songwriter's apartment building in New York City. Chapman's legal team first put forward a plea of insanity but, in June 1981, Chapman changed his mind and, saying that his actions had been the will of God, pleaded guilty. Convicted for second-degree murder, he was sentenced from 20 years to life and, as of 2016, has been denied parole nine times.

Police and Secret Service agents surge to disarm John Hinckley Jr. after his assassination attempt on Ronald Reagan in Washington, DC, in 1981.

Seventeen years later, in February 2003, the space shuttle *Columbia* disintegrated as it reentered the Earth's atmosphere. Again, all seven crew members died. This time, a suitcase-sized piece of foam insulation had broken off a rocket booster during the launch, puncturing a 6–10 inch (15–25 centimeter) hole in the orbiter's wing. Although this didn't affect the mission in space, when the orbiter returned to Earth, hot gases penetrated the wing, causing the spacecraft to become unstable and slowly break apart.

Suspended for more than two years, when the Space Shuttle Program relaunched, all subsequent missions, with one exception, were flown to the International Space Station, so that the crew could use it as a haven if similar damage to the orbiter prevented safe reentry.

COVERT OPERATIONS

Even as Reagan and Gorbachev were discussing the reduction in the numbers of their nuclear weapons, the Reagan administration was spending massively on arms, with the Defense Department's budget almost doubling between 1980 and 1985.

With the exception of CIA aid in opposing Cuban forces fighting in Angola in 1975–76, President Ford's and Carter's governments had been restrained in their involvement abroad. Reagan reversed this. The US now became active in a new Cold War battlefield—in Central America and the Caribbean. The 1983 military coup in Grenada provided the opportunity for a US military assault and occupation. Meanwhile, in Nicaragua, the CIA created and armed the anti-communist Contra rebel force, which succeeded in hampering the efforts of the country's socialist Sandinista government.

In November 1986, Reagan's administration was tainted by the revelation that the US had sold weapons to Iran, by then under the rule of fundamentalist Islamic clerics. Illegal under US law, the sale had been part of a much-denied deal to win the release of American hostages held in Lebanon. Furthermore, of the money received, $30 million had been diverted by National Security Council member Oliver North to fund the Contras in Nicaragua after Congress had cut off official funds for the rebels because of their appalling human rights record.

At first the president denied trading arms for hostages, but an investigation forced him to address the nation, admitting that that was exactly what he had done. Although weakened, Reagan's administration continued. A number of government and CIA staff were convicted of withholding evidence, though most were pardoned by Reagan's successor, President George H.W. Bush, in 1992.

THE END OF THE COLD WAR

By the late 1980s, the economic burdens in the Soviet bloc had become unsustainable, while Gorbachev's liberalizing policies were encouraging a "freedom of choice" among Warsaw Pact member states. When free elections in Poland and Hungary elected non-communist governments in 1989, the Soviet premier, unlike his predecessors, did not send in tanks to bring the countries back into line, but said that he would respect their decisions. Soon, mass protests swelled in East Germany against its hard-line communist government. When other Warsaw Pact countries opened their borders to the West, East Germany, already near bankruptcy, was left isolated. Nor did Gorbachev step in to save it. When East Germany lifted restrictions on travel on November 9, East Berliners flocked across the Berlin Wall and, over the following weeks, tore it down.

After 40 years, the Iron Curtain had been lifted. The American forces based in Western Europe had not gone into battle or fired their missiles. Having faced near war over the Cuban Missile Crisis, and fought proxy wars in Korea and Vietnam, America could watch as the Cold War ended peacefully. Within two years, though, interest would find a new focus of worry—in the Middle East, with American troops fighting in Iraq, the first of a number of conflicts in the region.

CHAPTER 3

THE SOLE SUPERPOWER

WITH THE SOVIET UNION BREAKING UP AFTER THE END OF THE COLD WAR, the US was left as the sole superpower. But with America becoming the target of Islamist terrorism and with instability in the Middle East, war and bloody conflict was not over for the United States.

In the 1980s, Iraq waged an eight-year war against Iran, only for it to end in stalemate, leaving a massive debt and mounting domestic discontent for its dictator, Saddam Hussein. His remedy was to attack another neighbor. This time it was the small emirate of Kuwait, the invasion of which increased his regional influence, gave him a victory to enjoy at last, and doubled his nation's oil reserves. He now controlled 20 percent of the world's oil.

However, this proved to be another miscalculation on Saddam's part. Although Iraq had received intelligence and equipment from the US, the United Kingdom, NATO, and other Arab states that were worried by the Islamic revolutionaries in Iran, invading Kuwait was regarded very differently. Kuwait, unlike Iran, was a small state on friendly terms with Western powers; within hours, the UN Security Council had condemned Iraq. Although some in Washington, such as the chairman of the Joint Chiefs of Staff, Colin Powell, hoped that sanctions would persuade Saddam to withdraw from Kuwait, President George H. W. Bush was keen to take military action, telling a conference, "We're dealing with Hitler revisited, a totalitarianism and a brutality that is naked and unprecedented in modern times."

Saddam's human rights abuses were indeed terrible. Human Rights Watch later estimated that 250,000 people had been murdered or had "disappeared" during Saddam's brutal dictatorship while, among many other offenses, the gassing of Kurds in the north of Iraq in 1988 had resulted in the deaths of at least 50,000 people. There was also the issue of Saddam's weapons of mass destruction (WMD). Chemical weapons had been used against Iran during the Iran–Iraq War, while biological weapons were being tested. Was Saddam planning to use these more widely?

THE GASSING OF KURDS IN THE NORTH OF IRAQ IN 1988 HAD RESULTED IN THE DEATHS OF AT LEAST 50,000 PEOPLE.

With a UN Security Council resolution secured, giving Saddam an ultimatum to withdraw from Kuwait by January 15, 1991, a US-led force of an international alliance was established. It included French and British forces, along with support from Saudi Arabia, Egypt, and—despite being no friend of America but close to Iran—Syria.

Following intensive bombing against Iraq's air defense and command systems in Iraq and Kuwait, ground operations—with 540,000 American troops and 250,000 from the other Allies—were launched from Saudi Arabia on February 24. Within 100 hours, Kuwait had been retaken. An estimated 35,000–80,000 Iraqi troops were killed, with 240 coalition soldiers lost. Almost a quarter of the American losses, and more than half of the British deaths, were a result of "friendly fire"—a feature of modern

The September 11 Memorial in New York City. The September 11 attacks in 2001 killed 2,996 people and injured more than 6,000 others. A new age of suicidal terrorism had reached the West.

warfare where long-range artillery and aircraft attack distant targets that they can't see.

Bush stopped the assault once Kuwait was liberated, despite criticism that he should have pressed on, invaded Iraq, and toppled Saddam. Writing seven years later, Bush defended his reasons for not invading Iraq, arguing that the international coalition would have immediately collapsed, and "the United States could conceivably still be an occupying power in a bitterly hostile land." He was right—as his son would find out a decade later.

THE BATTLE OF MOGADISHU

As part of a United Nations' operation to provide humanitarian aid and stabilize Somalia after it had fragmented into civil war in the early 1990s, the US Marines were sent to the country in 1992. The following October, a combination of various US special forces began a mission to capture leaders of the Habr Gidr clan in Somalia's capital, Mogadishu. With 19 aircraft, 12 vehicles, and 160 men, the operation was planned to take no more than an hour. In fact, the mission not only failed to capture its targets, but lasted for 15 hours after two Black Hawk helicopters were shot down, leaving the survivors isolated. As a fierce urban battle broke out, an immense combined task force of American, Malaysian, and Pakistani ground troops, along with armored vehicles and helicopters, was sent in to rescue the stranded soldiers.

In all, 18 US soldiers were killed and another 73 were wounded, with Malaysia and Pakistan also suffering a fatality each. The losses on the opposing side were immense, with the UN estimating that between 300 and 500 Somali fighters had been killed. The Battle of Mogadishu not only resulted in America scaling back its involvement in Somalia, but also cast a shadow over US foreign policy. Although President Bill Clinton's commitment of air power to the NATO bombing of Serb positions in 1999 during the Bosnian civil war did finally end a conflict that the UN and European Union had failed to resolve, America had not intervened in the Rwandan genocide in 1994.

A US soldier on patrol as part of a United Nations' force in Mogadishu, Somalia, in 1993. The failed US mission to capture Somali warlords that October was the bloodiest battle American troops had been involved in since the Vietnam War.

THE LOS ANGELES RIOTS

When 25-year-old African-American Rodney King was spotted speeding through the San Fernando Valley in the early hours of March 3, 1991, California Highway Patrol pursued him. King, who had been drinking, attempted to outrun them.

When finally cornered by the Los Angeles Police, King and his two passengers climbed out of the car. However, when King, who was unarmed, did not comply with the LAPD's requests to lie on the ground

A looted shop set on fire during the Los Angeles riots in April 1992. The riots erupted following the acquittal of four police officers who had been charged with—and had been filmed—assaulting African American Rodney King.

and instead attempted to flee, a vicious beating from the cops ensued, with King being hit 56 times. Caught on videotape by a local resident, the footage of the beating was later broadcast on a Los Angeles TV station, before building into a nationwide story of police brutality against an unarmed black man.

The four officers were charged with assault and using excessive force, but when they were acquitted at a trial the following April, parts of Los Angeles, centered around the African-American South Central area, erupted into six days of rioting. Apart from looting and arson, the violence, which was racially mixed, often targeted Hispanic and Korean communities. The Rodney King trial may have been the flashpoint but, more broadly, the rioting was attributed to the frustrations of poverty suffered during the early 1990s recession.

As rioting spread across the city, a curfew and the deployment of a federalized California Army National Guard eventually brought the situation under control, though by that time 55 people had been killed (10 by law enforcement agencies or the National Guard) and more than 2,000 injured.

A VICIOUS BEATING FROM THE COPS ENSUED, WITH KING BEING HIT 56 TIMES.

The following year, federal charges of civil rights violations were brought against the police officers who had beaten Rodney King, with two being found guilty and sentenced to 32 months in prison.

THE WACO SIEGE

David Koresh may have told his followers that he was God's prophet, that they must prepare for the end of days and that he had the right to procreate with any of his female followers—he fathered 22 children among the Branch Davidian sect's 100 members—but it was the build-up of illegal firearms at their communal home near Waco, Texas, that triggered the countdown to their apocalypse.

Following surveillance regarding the evidence of illegal firearms, on February 28, 1993, the Bureau of Alcohol, Tobacco, Firearms and Explosives (ATF) launched a raid on the Davidians' Mount Carmel Center. Reports differ over who fired first, but the Branch Davidians certainly proved to be highly armed—they were later found to have had 305 firearms, and in a two-hour gun battle, four officers and five sect members were killed.

A 51-day siege then ensued, with the FBI taking charge, cutting off water supplies and blasting loud music at the sect throughout the night.

Little progress was being made before, on April 19, tear gas was pumped into the compound. Six hours later and, it is believed, unrelated to the tear gas, three fires broke out inside the compound. Although there was enough time to flee, only nine members of the sect managed to escape the flames, with the other 76 dying in the fire.

The FBI's tactics were later criticized. In antagonizing the Branch Davidians, the argument went, the Bureau had fed into the sect's apocalyptic beliefs—and by the end Koresh thought that he was God—thus driving events towards a bloody climax rather than defusing the standoff.

OKLAHOMA CITY BOMBING

Two years to the day after the end of the siege at Waco, 26-year-old Timothy McVeigh detonated a car bomb in front of a federal building in Oklahoma City, killing 168 people, including 19 children, and injuring more than 600 others.

McVeigh had served in the US infantry during the First Gulf War, but, on leaving the army, had drifted, becoming increasingly alienated, touring gun shows and developing a loathing of what

David Koresh with a member of his Branch Davidians cult at their compound near Waco, Texas. When authorities attempted to raid the compound in February 1993, a siege began, ending 51 days later in a fire that killed 76 cult members.

he regarded as an increasingly socialist government. Deciding to target a federal building, McVeigh and his co-conspirator Terry Nichols built a 5,000 lb. (2,300 kg) bomb, which they mounted on the back of a truck. Lighting a two-minute fuse, McVeigh left the truck outside Oklahoma City's Alfred P. Murrah Federal Building. When tracked down, McVeigh claimed that his bombing was in revenge for the government's actions at Waco. Found guilty, among other charges, of using a weapon of mass destruction, he was executed by lethal injection in June 2001. Terry Nichols received a life sentence.

In April 1995, the bombing of a federal building in Oklahoma City killed 168 people. The bomber, Timothy McVeigh, claimed that his attack was in revenge for the government's handling of the Waco siege two years earlier.

O.J. SIMPSON

In the early 1990s, O.J. Simpson was a retired American football star and actor, most recently playing a goofy cop in The Naked Gun comedy films. Then, on the night of June 12, 1994, Simpson's ex-wife Nicole Brown and her friend, 25-year-old waiter Ron Goldman, were stabbed to death outside Brown's home in Los Angeles. Simpson was soon wanted on a double murder charge. No murder weapon has ever been found and there were no witnesses, but with blood samples and DNA evidence linking Simpson with the murders, the prosecution felt that it had a strong case. The defense team, however, managed to cast sufficient doubt over the DNA evidence—then a new science that few jurors understood fully—while also undermining the credibility of the LAPD. In anticipation of possible race riots if Simpson were found guilty, all LAPD officers were put on extended duty the day the verdict was announced. Simpson, however, was found not guilty in October 1995. The trials were not over for the star. In civil suits brought to court two years later, Simpson was found "responsible" for the murders, and the victims' families were awarded $33.5 million in compensatory and punitive damages.

The following decade, Simpson was involved in an armed robbery, burglary, and kidnapping while attempting to reacquire, in a Las Vegas hotel room, sports memorabilia that he claimed had been stolen from him. Found guilty, in 2008 he was sentenced to up to 33 years in prison. He was granted parole in July 2017.

THE WAR ON TERROR

In the twentieth century, airline crews were trained to stay calm and comply with hijackers' requests in order to see the plane landed safely at whichever airport the hijackers chose. The events of September 11, 2001 changed all that. Within 75 minutes, four American airliners on domestic flights from airports on the eastern seaboard were hijacked by terrorists and were crashed. The first two, 17 minutes apart, flew into the Twin Towers of the World Trade Center in New York, while the third hit the Pentagon Building outside Washington. Learning of these suicidal attacks, the passengers and flight attendants on the fourth plane realized that complying with hijackers would see them all killed. With the hijackers flying the plane towards Washington, DC, the passengers and flight attendants decided to fight back and attempted to storm the cockpit. In the struggle, the plane was brought down, crashing over Pennsylvania farmland and killing all on board.

The deadliest terrorist actions ever in America, the September 11 attacks killed 2,996 people and injured more than 6,000 others. Suspicion immediately fell on al-Qaeda, a network of radical Islamic fundamentalist cells co-founded by Saudi national, Osama bin Laden.

THE SEPTEMBER 11 ATTACKS KILLED 2,996 PEOPLE AND INJURED MORE THAN 6,000 OTHERS.

Originally allied with US-backed anti-communist forces, al-Qaeda had formed to counter the Soviet occupation in Afghanistan. At the time

The Pentagon in Virginia three days after a hijacked airliner was flown into the building on September 11, 2001. The attack killed all 64 people on board, as well as 125 on the ground.

HURRICANE KATRINA

The costliest natural disaster in the history of the United States, Hurricane Katrina caused severe destruction along the Gulf coast from Florida to Texas in August 2005. At least 1,245 people were killed in the storm and the ensuing floods. Much of the damage and loss of life occurred in New Orleans where, with levees breached in 50 places, 80 percent of the city was left underwater. The third most intense tropical cyclone to hit America, Katrina displaced more than one million people, causing the largest diaspora in US history.

While the Coast Guard, which had rescued 35,000 people, was recognized with an official entry in the Congressional Record, there was criticism of the broader response to the disaster, leading to the resignation of the Federal Emergency Management Agency director and the New Orleans Police Department superintendent. Investigations later found the US Army Corps of Engineers responsible for building inadequate flood defenses in New Orleans.

With levees breached in more than 50 places, 80 percent of New Orleans was flooded by the effects of Hurricane Katrina in August 2005.

of the September 11 attacks, its members were still being sheltered by Afghanistan's Islamic fundamentalist Taliban regime. Over the years, however, al-Qaeda had evolved to view the United States, with its forces in Saudi Arabia and its backing of conservative Middle Eastern states, as one of its enemies.

On September 20, President George W. Bush addressed Congress, using the term "war on terror" for the first time. This, he stated, would begin with al-Qaeda, but "will not end until every terrorist group of global reach has been found, stopped, and defeated." By Christmas 2001, the US, supported by British troops and Afghanistan's Northern Alliance, had removed the Taliban from power in Afghanistan. However, they had not captured Bin Laden, and the Taliban would eventually regroup. American forces, joined by those from 42 other NATO nations, would remain in Afghanistan.

WEAPONS OF MASS DESTRUCTION

In 1991, the first President Bush had likened Saddam to Hitler, and in 2002 his son described an "axis of evil," naming Iraq, Iran, and North Korea as three countries "arming to threaten the peace of the world. By seeking weapons of mass destruction, these regimes pose a grave and growing danger."

Regarding the September 11 attacks, there was no real evidence of Iraq sponsoring al-Qaeda, but George W. Bush was swept up in the idea of toppling Saddam. After Iraqi forces were defeated in Kuwait in 1991, there had been hopes in Washington that Shi'a Islam and Kurdish uprisings in Iraq would remove Saddam's minority Sunni Islam government, but the dictator had put them down viciously. Meanwhile, UN inspectors had been thwarted during the 1990s in their efforts to verify fully whether or not Iraq had developed any further weapons of mass destruction. Following a policy of containment, in 1998, America and Britain had bombed Iraqi military installations. However, apart from an intelligence claim that weapons of mass destruction were being developed, by February 2003, none had been found. As war approached, efforts were still being made to persuade Saddam to be fully transparent about the weapons but, not expecting to be invaded, he continued to play with and confuse the inspectors. The UK had wanted a UN resolution backing the use of force, but when the Security Council disagreed and that became impossible to achieve, the United States, supported by Britain, Spain, and Poland, invaded Iraq in March 2003. Within three weeks, Baghdad had fallen and by the end of the year Saddam had been captured. Occupation had been swift, with American casualties limited to 139. But after much searching, no weapons of mass destruction were ever discovered. For reasons of his personal hubris before the wider Arab world, Saddam had been bluffing.

What kind of peace would follow? Having neglected much in the way of planning what a post-Saddam Iraq would look like, a power vacuum developed after the dissolution of the country's largely Sunni Muslim army and the dismissal of government officials. Soon Sunni- and Iranian-backed Shi'a insurgent factions were battling each other and the occupying forces for dominance.

With a new constitution in 2005, parliamentary elections were held. After a trial, Saddam was found guilty of crimes against humanity and-hanged the following year. Despite efforts to wind down US involvement, however, an increase in sectarian violence led to more troops being deployed to Iraq in 2007. This was largely successful; two years later, the US handed security responsibilities to Iraqi forces. At the end of 2011, President Barack Obama withdrew American troops from Iraq.

There had been 4,804 deaths among 22 coalition military personnel, 4,486 of these being American. John Hopkins University estimated that the number of Iraqi deaths by 2011, both directly from violent action and indirectly through the breakdown of infrastructures, was 461,000. However, American involvement in Iraq was not yet over.

The South Tower (left) of the World Trade Center in New York seconds after a United Airlines 767 was flown into the building on the morning of September 11, 2001. A quarter of an hour earlier, an American Airlines 767 had been flown into the North Tower (right).

ENHANCED INTERROGATION

Within months of the invasion of Iraq in 2003, Amnesty International began reporting cases of human rights abuses involving torture and sexual humiliation carried out by US military police on Iraqi prisoners, most notoriously at Abu Ghraib Prison. The violations—sometimes proudly photographed—included physical and sexual abuse, rape, and murder. In defending their actions against charges of torture, sleep deprivation, and hooding, most of the abusers claimed that they were following orders and policy directions on interrogation methods. In addition to court martials and demotions, 11 American soldiers received prison sentences for the abuses, the longest being 10 years.

Some of the US policy about interrogation methods might not always have been clear, however. Shortly after the September 11 attacks, Vice President Dick Cheney had stated that in this new time of suicidal attacks, the government "needed to work through, sort of, the dark side" in combating the terrorists.

Although used on a limited basis by the CIA during the 1990s, it is believed that the practice of extraordinary rendition—of shackling and transporting terrorism suspects from one foreign state to another for interrogation—was expanded massively with the inception of the "war on terror." It has been alleged that hundreds of flights carried suspects across Europe and the Middle East to secret prisons, where they were tortured and held for months.

Some suspects were taken to the US base at Guantánamo Bay in Cuba where, beyond the jurisdiction of the territorial United States, a detention camp was established in 2002 that could hold prisoners without trial. More than 770 prisoners from more than 50 countries have been held at the camp, the highest proportion being Afghan, followed by Saudi, Yemeni, Pakistani, and other Asian, Middle Eastern, and European nationalities. President Obama repeatedly stated his desire to close Guantánamo. By 2016, the number of prisoners held at the camp had been reduced to 60, some being transferred to prisons in their home countries and some released. But with the US government considering the remaining prisoners too dangerous to release, while at the same time lacking sufficient admissible evidence to bring them to trial, the 60 prisoners held at Guantánamo remain in limbo.

FINDING BIN LADEN

At the time of the September 11 attacks, Osama bin Laden was believed to be living in Afghanistan. He would subsequently evade capture for many years, his whereabouts unknown. Almost a decade later, he was located living in a secure compound in the town of Abbottabad in Pakistan, about 100 miles (160km) from the Afghan border. On May 2, 2011, US Navy SEALs on two Black Hawk helicopters began an operation to kill him. Landing in the grounds of Bin Laden's compound, the SEALs fought their way through his house before finding the al-Qaeda leader. He and four members of his household were shot dead. Bin Laden's body was removed by US forces and given a Muslim burial at sea.

President Barack Obama and Secretary of State Hillary Clinton, along with members of the national security team, receive an update on the Navy SEALs' mission to assassinate Osama bin Laden in May 2011.

The memorial service for the five police officers who were shot in Dallas, Texas, by Micah Johnson in July 2016. They had been on duty at a Black Lives Matter protest about police killings of black men.

ISLAMIC STATE

As President Obama was attempting to reduce US presence in Iraq, unrest across the Middle East drew America and other countries into greater involvement in the region. In 2011, US air strikes as part of a NATO coalition force supported the toppling of dictator Colonel Gaddafi in Libya. Following the withdrawal of US troops in Iraq, the level of violence rose once again as militant groups fought, with Sunni groups attacking the country's Shi'a population and the Shi'a-led government.

In 2014, the fundamentalist Sunni Islam jihadist group Islamic State merged with its counterpart in the civil war in Syria to take control of towns in western and northern Iraq, including Fallujah and Mosul. Notorious for its beheadings of prisoners, public floggings, kidnappings and ethnic cleansing, Islamic State's advance prompted an increase in US military aid to the Iraqi government forces, with air attacks on Islamic State-held territory, as well as humanitarian aid drops. In 2015–16, with American and other coalition forces acting as advisers on the ground, the Iraq army succeeded in regaining ground taken by Islamic State jihadists.

Similarly, in Afghanistan, although security was transferred to Afghan forces with NATO troops largely having pulled out by the end of 2014, the US withdrawal slowed the following year as al-Qaeda tried to regroup in the area. With Islamic State becoming a presence there too, American forces remain in the country.

AT LIBERTY WITH GUNS

In Ferguson, Missouri, in August 2014, Michael Brown, an unarmed 18-year-old black man, was shot dead by a white police officer. In Louisiana in July 2016, Alton Sterling, also black, was shot dead while being pinned down by police, his gun still in his pocket. The following day in Minnesota, when challenged at a traffic stop, Philando Castile announced that he had a licensed gun in the car. Raising his hands, he was shot dead.

Following Castile's killing, there were both peaceful and violent protests in Minnesota state capital St. Paul against the police's perceived systemic racial violence. The following day, in Dallas, Texas, at a Black Lives Matter demonstration against police brutality, black gunman Micah Johnson shot dead five white police officers, before also being killed. Despite the headlines, some argue that incidents like the Sterling or Castile shootings do not reflect systemic racial violence among the police. When Harvard economist Roland G. Fryer Jr. examined data across a number of American cities, he found no evidence of racial discrimination in police shootings.

A pupil and her mother light a candle at the scene of the mass shootings at Sandy Hook Elementary School, Connecticut, December 2012.

Whether or not the police of all races are likely to shoot black people, there is a broader issue of gun crime among civilians in America, which perhaps says more about poverty and continued racial tension decades after the Civil Rights Movement. In Chicago in 2014, for instance, where the black and white populations are roughly equal in number, 2,460 black people were shot, lethally or non-lethally, compared with 78 white people. The American public is regularly shocked by mass shootings, such as that at Sandy Hook Elementary School in Newtown, Connecticut, in 2012, or at the Pulse nightclub in Orlando, Florida, in 2016. Responses vary from those who ask for stricter gun laws to those who call for more people to be armed so that they can fire back—although an FBI study found that in 160 incidents from 2000 to 2013, on only one occasion did armed members of the public stop a shooter.

Mass attacks, though, as shocking and extreme as they are, are not typical of most shootings. On average, 35 people in America are killed by guns every day, seven of them children. Usually the victims are poor and not white, unlike most of those killed and injured in mass school or college shootings.

ON AVERAGE, 35 PEOPLE IN AMERICA ARE KILLED BY GUNS EVERY DAY, SEVEN OF THEM CHILDREN.

America has the world's highest per capita gun ownership. There are more gun-related deaths in proportion to the population in the US than in Mexico. As gun violence continues to be prevalent in America, the debate around gun control will continue as well.

THE LAND OF OPPORTUNITY

It may seem a grim topic on which to end a history of America—even a bloody history—but these shootings and the debates around them reach to the core of what the United States is. As many pro-gun advocates argue, it is written in the Second Amendment, adopted in 1791, that "the right of the people to keep and bear arms shall not be infringed." Others counter that the Amendment says the arms are for "a well-regulated militia being necessary to the security of a free state;" that is, an organized military force, not armed individuals. Still others point out that even if the Second Amendment had meant individuals, it was written and agreed upon more than 200 years ago, in a world of slavery, in which there were no votes for women and when "arms" meant carrying a musket, not a submachine gun.

Beyond the different interpretations of the Second Amendment on an emotional level, is there some residue of the cowboy spirit, of the homesteader defending his property with his rifle, about America's relationship with firearms? The frontier may have gone, but, for better or worse, the rugged life of the West has become, for many Americans at least, part of their national identity.

In the world of industry and commerce, where the US has been so successful, firearms prove their mettle. In lobbying for gun rights, the National Rifle Association may champion civil liberties, but the very might of the NRA's campaigning, funded in part by gun manufacturers, is indicative of a very American characteristic—that of unfettered big business.

A demonstration in New York in June 2014 calling for stricter gun laws. America has the world's highest per capita gun ownership, with more gun-related deaths in proportion to population than Mexico.

Meanwhile, from state courts to the Supreme Court, laws on gun control are periodically tightened and relaxed, challenged and amended. For those people who have their bills defeated, it may seem an injustice, but this is American liberty at work—the liberty to lobby for these laws and to change them.

LAWS ON GUN CONTROL ARE PERIODICALLY TIGHTENED AND RELAXED, CHALLENGED AND AMENDED.

Emotionally and legally, America's gun laws embody ideas central to the identity of the United States—that neither individuals nor states can be unduly limited by an overreaching federal government. That was key to the Founding Fathers' belief laid down in the Tenth Amendment in the Bill of Rights.

If enough Americans wanted to amend the Second Amendment, they could. Prohibition was introduced by one amendment in 1919, and repealed by another in 1933. That such strong, opposing views are held about gun laws is evidence of the success of the United States as a democracy, with a government, as Abraham Lincoln said at the Gettysburg Address, "of the people, by the people, for the people."

REALITY TV PRESIDENCY

"He has neither the temperament nor the judgment to be president." These were the words of Republican Mitt Romney, spoken, not about a Democrat opponent, but about Donald Trump, his own party's candidate in the 2016 presidential election. That was in March 2016. Eight months later, before the election, more than 160 other senior Republicans had announced that they, too, would not be supporting Trump. This was clearly going to be a very divisive election.

But then Trump is a very unusual figure. Like a contestant on reality TV—the genre that, tellingly, turned him into a star—the billionaire property developer drew huge attention on the campaign trail by saying much that was outrageous, and to many, offensive. His aggressive election

The 45th president of the United States, Donald Trump, is the first to never have held public office or to have served in the military. Even before he entered the White House, Trump had made history.

speeches grabbed headlines with his slurs—stating that many Mexican immigrants were rapists, criminals, and drug mules, saying there should be a temporary shutdown on all Muslims entering the US, and claiming that his opponent, Hillary Clinton, was "crooked."

He enraged many, but Trump's "Make America great again" populist campaign resonated with others, crucially white, blue-collar workers in the "rust belt" states, where families still struggle after the 2008 financial crash. With parts of the electorate disenchanted with Establishment politics as embodied by Clinton, outsider Trump represented change. But what kind of change would it be? Could the wounds of the most bitter election in more than a century be easily healed? Which way would a divided America now turn?

The Freedom Wall at the National World War II Memorial, Washington, DC. The wall features 4,048 gold stars, each representing 100 Americans who died in the conflict. At the front is a message that reads: "Here we mark the price of freedom."

GLORY, HALLELUJAH

The history of America has been bloody, but that doesn't mean that it has always been shameful. It was bloody conflict that threw off the shackles of British rule in the Revolutionary War to create the United States; it was bloody conflict that held the Union together and ended slavery in the Civil War; and it was by going to war that fascism was defeated in World War II. Furthermore, the nonviolent Freedom Riders of the Civil Rights movement knew that they were courting violence in the fight against segregation and discrimination.

America may be criticized for its persecution of its native people or for its imperialism, but these accusations can be leveled at many other countries, too. Perhaps it is preferable to consider the valor of the volunteers and conscripts who have served America, from Iraq and Afghanistan to Vietnam and Korea, from the world wars to the Civil War and back to the Revolutionary War. Better to remember the bravery of the Civil Rights activists, of the soldiers raising the flag at Iwo Jima, and of the young men landing on the beaches of Normandy at D-Day, and to honor those who fell at Shiloh, Yorktown, Saratoga, and in many other conflicts.

GLOSSARY

acquiescing Submitting to or accepting something, despite hesitation, without opposition.

Agent Orange A defoliating chemical, which is harmful to leaves and plant life, often causing deforestation and general harm to the land, used in the Vietnam War.

Berlin Wall The wall that once divided East Germany and West Berlin to control the migrant population.

coup An upheaval or overturning, particularly that of authority or leadership.

guerrilla A person who uses hit-and-run tactics, manipulating chaos, sabotage, and constant hindrance, such as in guerrilla warfare.

Iron Curtain A term coined by Winston Churchill as a metaphorical image for a barrier of isolation—referring particularly to that of the Soviet Union on the Eastern Bloc and its governments.

moratorium A period of delay or forbiddance set in place by some legal authority.

terrorist A person who employs terror, involving violence and the spread of fear, to advance political goals.

Tet Offensive An attack during a temporary truce for Vietnam's New Year holiday of Tet, when the NVA and the Viet Cong launched major assaults on cities and towns all over the South resulting in an influential blow to support for the war in America while it was reported on American television news every night.

Viet Cong The guerrilla soldiers who fought for Vietnam in the Vietnamese Communist movement.

Watergate Referring to the scandal surrounding the Watergate Hotel, which president Richard Nixon resigned over when it was discovered he was directly involved with the five operatives attempting to bug the Democratic National Committee.

FOR MORE INFORMATION

American Psychological Association
750 First Street Northeast
Washington, DC 20002-4242
(800) 374-2721
Website: *http://www.apa.org/index.aspx*
This association studies psychology and psychological trends on international and national scales.

Canadian Museum of Human Rights
85 Israel Asper Way
Winnipeg, MB R3C 0L5, Canada
(877) 877-6037
Website: *https://humanrights.ca/*
Canada's museum on the history of human rights, detailing both violations and advancements in the past and still to come.

Canadian War Museum
1 Vimy Place
Ottawa, ON K1A 0M8, Canada
(819) 776-7000
Website: *http://www.warmuseum.ca/*

A globally reputed museum for its study and research on the history of armed conflict.

National Consortium for the Study of Terrorism and Responses to Terrorism (START).
University of Maryland, College Park
8400 Baltimore Ave, Suite 250
College Park, MD 20740
(301) 405-6600
Website: *http://www.start.umd.edu/*
The START program researches the many aspects of modern terrorism in the United States.

New-York Historical Society
170 Central Park West at Richard Gilder Way (77th Street)
New York, NY, 10024
(212) 873-3400
Website: *http://www.nyhistory.org/*
New York's historical society devoted to research, art, exhibits, education, and the preservation of history.

9/11 Memorial Museum
180 Greenwich Street
New York, NY, 10007
(212) 312-8800
Website: *https://www.911memorial.org/*
This museum preserves the story of the September 11 attacks and acts as a memorial to those who lost their lives.

FURTHER READING

Appy, Christine G. *American Reckoning: The Vietnam War and Our National Identity*. New York, NY: Penguin Books, 2016.

Bingham, Clara. *Witness to the Revolution: Radicals, Resisters, Vets, Hippies, and the Year America Lost Its Mind and Found Its Soul*. New York, NY: Random House, 2016.

Dancis, Bruce. *Resister: A Story of Protest and Prison during the Vietnam War*. Ithaca, NY: Cornell University Press, 2014.

Dean, John W., and James Robenalt Jr. *January 1973: Watergate, Roe v. Wade, Vietnam, and the Month That Changed America Forever*. Chicago, IL: Chicago Review Press, 2015.

Hayden, Michael V. *Playing to the Edge: American Intelligence in the Age of Terror*. New York, NY: Penguin Press, 2016.

Lowery, Wesley. *They Can't Kill Us ALL: Ferguson, Baltimore, and a New Era in America's Racial Justice Movement*. New York, NY: Little, Brown and Company, 2016.

Mandelbaum, Michael. *Mission Failure: America and the World in the Post-Cold War Era*. New York, NY: Oxford University Press, 2016.

Means, Howard. *67 Shots: Kent State and the End of American Innocence*. Boston, MA: Da Capo Press, 2016.

Mitchell, Greg. *The Tunnels: Escapes Under the Berlin Wall and the Historic Films the JFK White House Tried to Kill*. New York, NY: Crown, 2016.

INDEX

T

U

V

W